Textiles from Medieval Egypt, A.D. 300–1300

Thelma K. Thomas
The University of Michigan

with Glossary by
Deborah G. Harding
The Carnegie Museum
of Natural History

The Carnegie Museum of Natural History

This publication was made possible through a grant from the National Endowment for the Humanities, a federal agency.

Published by The Carnegie Museum of Natural History, Pittsburgh, PA 15213
ISBN 0-911239-20-0
Library of Congress Catalog Card Number: 89-85825

Cover drawing: Garment fragment of tapestry from the Byzantine period showing a leopard. See also figure 9.

Contents

About the Authors

Thelma K. Thomas is lecturer in the Department of History of Art and assistant curator of collections at The Kelsey Museum of Ancient and Mediaeval Archaeology at the University of Michigan. A graduate of Bryn Mawr College and candidate for the Ph.D. from New York University, she has received many awards and fellowships for studies in Egyptian and Byzantine art. She has lectured and published on these subjects and curated exhibitions for several museums.

Deborah G. Harding, who wrote the Glossary for this booklet, is collection manager for the Division of Anthropology of The Carnegie Museum of Natural History. She is a graduate of Beloit College, Beloit, Wisconsin, and is currently a student in the Ph.D. program of the Department of Anthropology of the University of Pittsburgh. She has worked extensively with various textiles in museum settings and has been a weaver for twenty years.

Preface

The Carnegie Museum of Natural History possesses a fine and extensive collection of textiles from medieval Egypt. Most of the five hundred textiles, from the collection of the Swedish archaeologist F. R. Martin, were purchased by the museum in the 1930s under the directorship of A. Avinoff. The collection comprises both complete and fragmentary articles of clothing and furnishings dating from Egypt's Byzantine and Islamic periods. Some of the textiles are of exceptional quality; others are important examples of rare techniques, styles, or images; a few are, to my knowledge, unique. This publication, which presents selected examples in the text and in Appendix 2, introduces the collection to both the interested public and specialists in the field.

Thanks to Egypt's dry climate, there exists a nearly unbroken record of textile remains from ancient to modern times. Textiles from medieval Egypt, preserved in great numbers, reflect the changing conditions under which textiles were produced and used. They also reflect the momentous political, cultural, and religious upheavals Egypt experienced during the Middle Ages: Ancient pagan ways were gradually abandoned as the country was officially converted first, under Byzantine rule, to Christianity and then, under the Arab dynasties, to Islam.

Discoverers of these textiles—including amateur archaeologists at the turn of the century and dealers in antiquities—often quite casually excavated whole cemeteries within a single season as they looked for Pharaonic remains, meanwhile destroying the funerary settings in which the textiles were discovered (see figure 1). Corollary evidence which could have provided valuable information for dating these textiles (coins and written documents, for example) was not recorded before the textiles were dispersed to museum and private collections around the world. As a consequence, attempting to assign dates to the scattered, and usually fragmentary, works presents a serious problem for present-day historians.

Textile remains from burials should be interpreted with caution. They do not accurately illustrate all aspects of textile manufacture and use because they were not always the furnishings or clothes used during daily life. Burial conditions soiled and promoted the disintegration of the textiles, in part, by contact with decaying corpses. In addition, the decorated portions of the more interesting fabrics were very often cut out of the garments or furnishings for which they were made (as illustrated in several figures in this booklet), so that

*1. This 1902 etching shows
the excavation of a
Byzantine period cemetery
at Antinoë (Antinoopolis) in
Upper Egypt. The
excavations were undertaken
by the French archaeologist
A. Gayet.*

collectors took only the most appealing parts. Fortu-
nately, the types of textiles and their wider historical
settings are often illuminated by visual records (paintings, sculptures, etc.) and an abundance of primary
written sources. The surviving examples and the written remains indicate that the textiles from medieval
Egypt were the products of international manufacture
and trade and that the textile industry was one of the
most important industries of the medieval period in
the Mediterranean regions (see figure 2).

The basic technologies were developed first in ancient Egypt and adapted in later periods when the
expansion of trade under a succession of foreign rulers

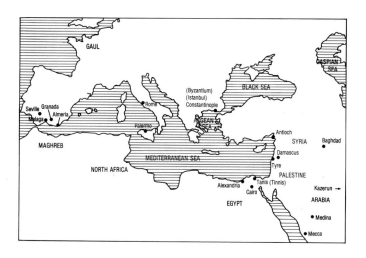

2. *Mediterranean regions in*
the Middle Ages.

widened the availability of materials and fashions. This booklet begins with a brief summary of the earlier Pharaonic, Greek, and Roman textile traditions in order to clarify the continuing importance of technical, artistic, and cultural traditions in medieval Egyptian textiles. Textiles and textile traditions of the Byzantine and Islamic periods are discussed in the following sections. For more information the reader may refer to the maps in the text and to the appendices, glossary of technical terms, and suggestions for further reading at the end of this booklet.

Pre-Byzantine Textile Traditions

Materials, Their Qualities, and Values. A variety of fibers were used in textiles produced during Egypt's

Pharaonic period. Linen, woven of threads spun from flax, was the predominant textile fiber used in Predynastic and Pharaonic Egypt. Tough, durable, and tremendously variable, linen was manufactured in four grades of quality from a fine translucent gauze bleached white to a course thick canvas in natural tans and light browns. Wool, shorn from goats and sheep, was also widely produced for clothing and furnishings, and was cheaper than linen but of lower quality. Coir-type fibers (grass, reeds, hemp) were also woven and plaited for mats, baskets, and so forth. Dyes* were produced from organic materials such as plants and from inorganic materials such as earths.

In ancient Egypt, the finest linens were reserved through state monopolies for royalty, nobility, and the priestly class, whereas the thicker grades were commonly available at lower prices. Wool was also in widespread use for clothing and furnishings, such as curtains, wall hangings, pillowcovers, and blankets. During the Ptolemaic and Roman periods, cotton and silk were introduced into Egypt via expanded trade routes to the East.

Ancient patterned textiles and linens were valuable, and thus were stored carefully, mended, darned, and handed down as heirlooms. Linen scraps were not discarded but were reused, often as mummy wrappings. Pharaonic textiles were bartered for commodities through international trade. During the Ptolemaic and Roman periods, patterned textiles remained costly because they were still produced by labor-intensive work. Highly prized, they were given in dowries, handed down as heirlooms, offered as gifts for temples, or converted to cash if the need arose. Linen continued

*See Glossary when a word is followed by an asterisk.

as the most common fabric for clothing, mummy wrappings and shrouds, and domestic furnishings in Egypt during the Ptolemaic period. Silk was extremely expensive, literally worth its weight in gold. It was bought as whole cloth, but Greek women often rewove and embroidered* it to suit their own tastes and utilized it, for example, for decorative effects on cuffs and collars, rather than fashioning entire garments out of silk.

In ancient Egypt, quality of material and clothing type indicated one's socioeconomic status. During the Pharaonic period, an increasing elaborateness in ornament and cut also indicated higher ranks. Conversely, the scantier the garment, the humbler the wearer's status was likely to be.

The Greeks introduced new fashions in clothing which also distinguished different levels of society. Greek and Greco-Egyptian children wore smaller, shorter versions of adult garb. Common among the upper classes of men and women was the Greek ensemble of a *chiton* (tunic) of lightweight linen under a *himation* (mantle) of wool or linen and wool. Both garments were colorful, often ornamented with stripes of different colors, all-over patterns, and/or inserts of brightly colored tapestry-woven* and embroidered designs.

When the rule of Egypt passed into the hands of the Roman emperors, a new set of fashions more precisely indicative of age, citizenship, and social status entered Egypt with its new Roman administrators. The toga was the proper ordinary dress for the Roman citizen. During the first centuries of Roman rule, tunics continued to be worn by those men who were not citizens, the workers (or plebeians). The tunic was usually of plain wool or linen and in some cases decorated with one stripe (*clavus**) down the center front and back, or

a   b

3. (a) A Roman period short, knee-length tunic with sleeves extending to the elbow. This garment was the daily dress of citizens and plebeians (those who did not belong to the higher social and governing orders). (b) The formal and official civilian dress of a Roman citizen—the toga—was worn over a tunic. The elaborately draped garment, which was semicircular, was folded along its length and placed over the left shoulder. In this drawing, a pocket has been formed in the front.

two *clavi* down the sides of the front and back. Earlier, these *clavi* had been military insignia, but by the second century A.D., when the tunic supplanted the toga as the ordinary dress of citizens (see figure 3), the insignia had lost their symbolic significance and became purely decorative. The insignia were tapestry-woven into the material in wools of purple, indigo, or a deep wine color (see figure 4). Both *tunica*† and *colobia*, a short-sleeved variety of the tunic, were worn by men from the first century B.C. into the third century A.D. Women, who

6 †Latin for "tunics."

4. *A garment fragment showing a medallion encircling a star and decorated with geometric interlaced patterns. It is tapestry-woven* with purple wool threads with flying shuttle* work in undyed linen against a background of plainwoven undyed linen. Size, 21 × 19 cm (mended). Byzantine or later (?). Provenience unknown. CMNH 10309-22.*

were not citizens, wore garments of the same patterns as the Greek *chiton* and *himation*, known by their Roman names, *stola* (tunic) and *pallium* (cloak). A border at the bottom of the *stola* was reserved for matrons.

Tools, Techniques, and Workers. Ancient Egyptian, Greek, and Roman cloth-making technologies were similar (see Glossary: Looms). All weaves, even the most complex, were variations of the simple, or tabby,* weave in which there is a ratio of one vertical or warp* thread to one horizontal or weft* thread. The simple weave was commonly used for garments and for mummy wrappings. Textures of simple-woven linens were sometimes varied by crimping or pleating, which was done while the textile was wet, either on specially made boards or by hand. For decorative bands, polychrome (or multicolored) geometric patterns were created by alternating differently colored weft threads. Tapestry weave, found only in the most elaborately decorated fabrics, used discontinuous weft threads of different colors, alternately taken up and dropped within a row of warp threads to create multicolored patterns of geometric, abstract, figural, or symbolic designs.

Pharaonic textiles were manufactured commercially by state-employed workers of both sexes and all ages (including children) in royal workshops, sometimes attached to temples, or in home-based industries. Similarly, during the Ptolemaic period, professional weavers were men, women, and children, both trained slaves and freely employed, working in factories and in private homes. Some Greek entrepreneurs in Egypt, both men and women, came to own many profitable textile businesses in different locations. In time-hallowed Greek tradition, respectable Greek women spun and wove wool in the home; working in wool was a Greek woman's only substantial contribution to the household economy. After the fourth century B.C., however, Greek women were no longer so strictly confined to the home and embarked upon other careers. At that point, Greek men transformed the craft into an industry, making textiles commercially available. In Egypt, where men had always been involved with the commercial production of textiles, this was not the innovation it was in Greek lands; but Greek women continued to work in wool in their Egyptian homes, performing with the help of domestic servants (and, infrequently, slaves) all chores related to clothing production, from preparing the wool to sewing the garments.

During the Roman period, textiles continued to be manufactured by professionals in businesses, on private estates, and domestically. Greek and hellenized Egyptian women continued to weave in the home. Ancient production practices, weaving techniques, and the repertory of garment types remained in use throughout the Byzantine period.

The Byzantine Period

At the beginning of the fourth century A.D., the Roman emperor Constantine established an eastern capital of the Empire in a Greek town on the Bosphoros, Byzantium, which he renamed Constantinople (present-day Istanbul). By far the most significant change to the character of the Eastern Roman, or Byzantine, Empire was its official conversion to Christianity. As the Empire gradually converted, Christians with their monotheistic traditions came to coexist alongside followers of the polytheistic religions practiced in its many countries.

Egypt was a part of the Byzantine Empire during the fourth, fifth, and sixth centuries A.D. This was the period of the growth and development of the principal forms of Catholicism: Greek orthodoxy promoted by the Byzantine emperors, Roman Catholicism spreading among the fragmentary societies of western Europe, and, in the middle of this period, the Eastern Orthodox Churches of Syria, Armenia, and Egypt, the last of which came to be known as the Coptic Church. (The religious and cultural designation, Coptic, has also been applied to the arts of Egypt during this period.)

The Textile Industry. During Egypt's Byzantine period, textile manufacture continued along the lines of preexisting Egyptian, Greek, and Roman technical and artistic traditions. Dyeing and weaving, for example, were practiced domestically and commercially by specialists of both sexes who learned their craft through long apprenticeships as in the earlier Roman period. Professional weavers plied their trades in government-controlled factories, in privately owned workshops, and as itinerants. They were severely restricted by early Byzantine law, as were most trained craftsmen. Their status was particularly low, and they were constantly reminded of that by laws governing such aspects of their lives as their marriage and the status of their children. Wages were fixed and a change of professions was not allowed. Thus, except for trained slaves and women working in the home, professions were established at the time of birth by inheritance (except in the rarest of instances). Dyers, working under similar restrictions, had an equally low status.

Apart from the straits of its workers, the textile industry flourished in Egypt under Byzantine rule. Businessmen and women involved in textile production and commerce prospered. The Byzantine government attempted, with limited success, to impose regulations on textile production in all its territories. State factories took legal priority over the needs and demands of private enterprises. Trade between foreign textile centers within the vast confines of the Empire and an edict setting maximum prices also affected Egyptian textile workers, middlemen, and patrons. Because of expanded trade with India and China, there was a gradual increase in the importation of both cotton and silk, but linen and wool continued to be the most common fabrics for clothing and furnishings.

The major Egyptian centers of textile production seem to have been located along the length of the Nile Valley and across the Delta at important Greek and Roman cities, evidently continuing from the previous Greek and Roman periods (see figure 5). Extensive textile trade occurred within Egypt's own borders, sometimes on an intimate first-name basis. This is seen, for example, in an early Byzantine "Private Letter" from Egypt:

> To Hermammon, greetings from Longinus . . . we
> salute you from Pelusium. . . . Be kind enough,
> if the clothes have arrived, to supply my young
> brother with a pair not of the fleecy variety but of
> the other sort, smooth and embroidered; take the
> money for them from him—I've provided him with
> it. . . . Be of good heart, remember us as we re-
> member you, and for this reason that we shall take
> thought for you. Boethus the embroiderer greets
> you. (*The Antinoopolis Papyri. Part II*, 1950, vol. 1:
> 101–02)

Types of Textiles. Domestic furnishings, we know from written sources, were of the same types as those of the Roman and Ptolemaic periods—pillows, mattresses, coverings, blankets, and so forth—but were not usually preserved in the funerary settings in which

11

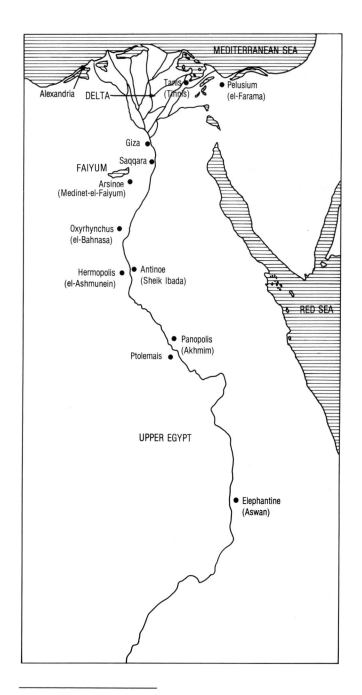

MEDITERRANEAN SEA

Alexandria

DELTA

Tanis
(Tinnis)

● Pelusium
(el-Farama)

Giza ●

FAIYUM

Saqqara ●

Arsinoe ●
(Medinet-el-Faiyum)

Oxyrhynchus ●
(el-Bahnasa)

Hermopolis ● ● Antinoe
(el-Ashmunein)   (Sheik Ibada)

RED SEA

Panopolis
(Akhmim)

Ptolemais ●

UPPER EGYPT

● Elephantine
(Aswan)

— *5. Chief discovery sites of*
12 *Byzantine textiles in Egypt.*

6. *A fragment from a wall hanging that has a subtly shaded column, with a Doric capital and part of the cornice preserved, and a fruit-laden vine. It is tapestry-woven with wool threads dyed yellow, black, white, pink, orange, red (background), and blue-green (warp*).*

Size, 28 × 19 cm. Byzantine or later (?). Provenience unknown. CMNH 10061-169.

most of the textiles have been discovered. Textile furnishings, depending on use and value, may have borne tapestry-woven, embroidered, or resist-dyed decoration. Although secular and pagan designs were frequently used in these early textiles, Christian imagery increasingly gained in popularity, paralleling Egypt's conversion to Christianity (see figures 6 and 7).

Churches were also furnished with textiles. Usually highly valued donations (like those textiles in pagan temples), these textiles were of many different types: either plain or decorated with Christian motifs, whether a simple cross, holy figures, or elaborate narrative sequences illustrating the Scriptures. A Byzantine-period "Inventory of Church Property" from Egypt, for example, lists among furniture and liturgical utensils the following types of textiles (without, unfortunately, any indications of the designs they might have had): two hangings, twenty-three linen cloths for the altar slab, five woolen cloths, six door curtains and other cloths specified as old, one hanging

7. *This garment fragment of undyed linen has a* clavus* *decorated with a geometric interlaced pattern and crosses. Its borders are ornamented with vegetal motifs, a wavecrest pattern, and circles. It is tapestry-woven with dark purple wool with flying shuttle work in undyed linen.*

Size, 23 × 22 cm. Byzantine or later (?). Provenience unknown. CMNH 10309-34.

woolen curtain, one hanging cover, and one "triply-woven web" (Hunt and Edgar, 1932: 432–35).

The types of garments worn during Egypt's Byzantine period are well known. After a law introduced in the fourth century prohibited the practice of mummification, the dead came to be buried in lavish examples of garments worn during life. Changes in the styles and ornaments of these garments are described in documents of the period as having been influenced by politics and religion.

Imperial dress and regalia, based on Roman period garment types, underwent symbolic changes during the Byzantine period. Generally, the styles became more conspicuously sumptuous. Specifically, silk, Tyrian purple dye, and gold threads were deliberately invested with imperial significance as, throughout this period, numerous laws were introduced to restrict their use. Only the emperors' entrances and exits (with clothing changes in between) could be dramatic shimmering displays of silk, purple, and gold that left no doubt in the minds of the viewers as to who was at the top of the political and economic hierarchy.

Silk manufacture was controlled by the Byzantine state. The Byzantine historian Procopius recorded how sericulture (the production of raw silk by raising silkworms) came to the Empire toward the end of this period, in A.D. 552, when two Christian monks of Persian origin smuggled silkworm eggs out of China in hollowed walking sticks and brought them to the emperor Justinian. Procopius also records that Justinian established imperial factories, called *"gynacea"* (Greek for "women's quarters"; here the Greek heritage is doubly clear). It has been suggested that the major Egyptian *gynaceum* for producing silk was at Alexandria.

Some aspects of the silk industry were prohibitively expensive, affordable only by the nearly inexhaustible imperial coffers. The deepest and clearest purple dye for silk, for example, was found in one location off the shore of Tyre in Syria within the shell of a particular type of mollusk. Enormous quantities of mollusks were needed to produce small amounts of the dye; and the mollusks themselves accounted for only one part of this large-scale operation including off-shore boats, netters, and divers for gathering the mollusks; vats for boiling them in order to produce the dye; and expanses of empty coastline for drying the dyed silks.

There was, moreover, a special office charged with the keeping of the silks owned by the emperors. In their donations of silks to Western rulers who had little or no trade with China, Byzantine emperors reinforced popular Western notions that this fine glistening cloth was not made by human hands, but was divinely or magically created. The emperors also bestowed silken regalia, usually pallia or mantles, upon their appointed officials.

Private fashions imitated Byzantine imperial styles in elaborateness as well as in colors and materials. Men and women went to frivolous extremes in aping imperial opulence as elaborate figured decorations became popular in tapestry-woven clothing (see figures 8–10). Along with other religious figures, Asterius, the Bishop of Amaseia of Syria in the late fourth and early fifth century A.D., sermonized heatedly against the "fashion victims" who wore such garments:

> They have invented some kind of vain and curious warp and broidery which, by means of the interweaving of warp and weft, imitates the quality of painting and represents upon garments the forms of all kinds of living beings, and so they devise for themselves, their wives and children gay-colored dresses decorated with thousands of figures. . . . When they come out in public dressed in this fashion, they appear like painted walls to those they meet. They are surrounded by children who laugh among themselves and point out their fingers at the pictures on the garments. . . . You may see lions and leopards, bears, bulls and dogs, forests and

8. A piece of mesh fabric in sprang* technique done in a geometric pattern based on paired curving diagonal and interlaced vertical lines. The threads are wool dyed dark blue (background), gold (lines), and red (dots in interstices of interlace). It is almost completely preserved, with a selvedge* at the top and gathering at the bottom to create a bag that has the same design on either side.

Size, 24 × 58 cm. Byzantine or later (?). Provenience unknown. CMNH 28448-8.

9. A garment fragment
showing a leopard in a
medallion, from a set of
medallions and clavi
decorating a dalmatic. It is
tapestry-woven with dark
brown wool threads against

a background of undyed
linen.

Size, 6 cm diameter.
Byzantine. Provenience
unknown. CMNH 10309-47.

rocks, hunters and [in short] the whole repertory
of painting that imitates nature. . . . The more religious among rich men and women, having picked
out the story of the Gospels, have handed it over to
the weavers—I mean our Christ together with all
his disciples, and each one of the miracles the way
it is related. . . . In doing this they consider them-

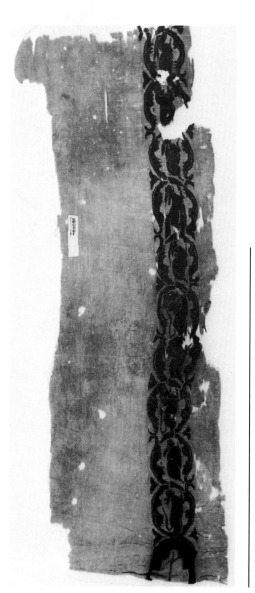

10. A clavus from a
dalmatic, decorated with
animals in a vine rinceau.*
It is tapestry-woven with
dark brown wool against a
background of undyed linen.

Size, 21.5 × 55 cm.
Byzantine. Provenience
unknown. CMNH 10309-88.

selves to be wearing clothes that are agreeable to God. If they accepted my advice, they would sell those clothes and honor instead the living images of God. Do not depict Christ . . . but bear in your spirit and carry about with you the incorporeal Logos [i.e., the spiritual word of God]. Do not display the paralytic on your garments, but seek out him who lies ill in bed. (Mango, 1972: 50–51)

Asterius, incidentally, also offers us a clue as to how such a wide variety of patterns came to be preserved among such a limited selection of the textiles in use during this time: The patrons created their own designs which the weaver recreated in cloth. Thus, in addition to depicting variations on the generic motifs commonly employed in the weaving establishments, clothing decoration could make clear personal, religious, and political statements. Although Asterius' main concern was to stop excessive expenditures for clothing and to exhort his congregation to lead a wholly Christian way of life, his sermon had a political subtext as well. In another passage of the sermon quoted above, Asterius allied himself with imperial regulations when he warned against the private use of silk and Tyrian purple dye. Throughout the Byzantine period, however, in spite of stiff penalties and opprobrium, legal and religious prohibitions against production and consumption were not strictly followed. There were, of course, less-expensive and simpler garments for those with less ostentatious personalities or lesser means.

At the beginning of the Byzantine period, a new variant on the tunic was introduced into men's wardrobes. Named after the country of its origin, Dalmatia (modern Yugoslavia), the dalmatic became common everyday clothing for men of most social and economic levels. Cut much wider and longer than the

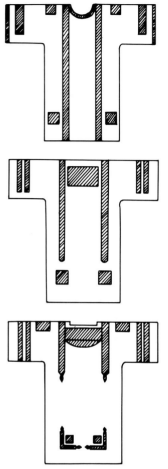

11. The early Byzantine tunic, or dalmatic, was, frequently, richly ornamented with stripes and patches of various shapes. The types of decoration shown here are clavi, *pairs of panels at shoulder or knees, L-shaped bands, sleevebands, and neckbands.*

old Roman style of tunic, the dalmatic was decorated with patches of similar patterns found throughout the Empire (see figure 11). Similar to the Roman tunic, the dalmatic was ornamented with purple stripes or *clavi* and patches (not the famous Tyrian purple but a cheaper mixture of red and blue vegetable dyes) sometimes highlighted in yellow (also from vegetable dyes) in linen and wool. The early Byzantine dalmatic may have had geometric or figural motifs (see figures 12 and 13).

The toga, retained as the ceremonial costume of

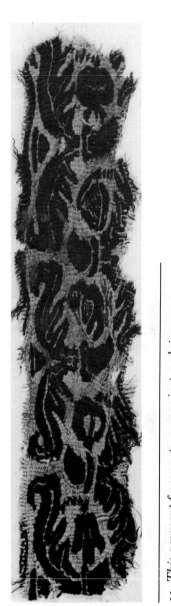

12. This garment fragment has a band decorated with a duck and plants within a vine rinceau. It is tapestry-woven with purple and red (beak, legs, and feet) wools against a plainwoven background of undyed linen.

Size, 5.3 × 23.5 cm. Byzantine. Provenience unknown. CMNH 10309-42.

13. A star-shaped shoulder patch. The points of the star are made by a square decorated with a geometric interlace pattern overlapping another square decorated with leaves at the four corners. The patch is attached to a clavus that has a leaf pendant. This piece is tapestry-woven with purple wool with flying shuttle work in linen against a plainwoven background of undyed linen.

Size, 22.5 × 58.8 cm. Byzantine or later (?). Provenience unknown. CMNH 10309-84.

senators during the early Byzantine period, was longer and narrower and more elaborately draped than its Roman period models (see figure 14). Again, there were legal restrictions on ceremonial costume for those of highest ranks and on clothing for those of the lowest in order to honor specific occasions appropriately and as indications of status. For example, an early Byzantine law on "The Garb which must be worn within the City" gave specific instructions about the required apparel for Senators, their attendants, and slaves, and outlined the punishment for disregarding the statute (Pharr, 1952: 415). Dress regulations also reflected the political concerns of the Byzantine emperors because foreign fashions could be read as statements of political alliances.

The extent of a man's wardrobe depended on imperial regulations, status, budgetary restrictions, and personal inclinations. Commonly, lightweight whites and natural tans were worn during the summer; heavier garments of darker colors, along with shawls and socks, were worn in the winter.

The surviving textile remains (and artistic representations) indicate that respectable women of means wore long wide garments, *colobia*, belted high up above the waist, often over long-sleeved inner tunics (see figure 15). These were simply cut, often ornamented with stripes of embroidery or tapestry-woven designs. Texts of the period inform us that women's wardrobes were subject to the same kinds of restrictive imperial legislation as were those of men. Legal prohibitions against actresses, who were by no means considered to be respectable women, suggest that they were noticeably (flamboyantly?) ignoring the clothing laws addressed to the general population.

Children wore smaller, often simpler, versions of

14. The last form of toga, used as a ceremonial costume of Byzantine consuls. Here, the elaborately decorated toga is worn over a ⁷/₈-length colobium which is worn over a full-length tunic decorated with clavi.

15. These drawings (after portraits from the Roman catacombs) show the very full, early Byzantine dalmatic in varying widths and lengths worn by women (who are in the posture assumed while praying— standing, with arms outstretched and raised up, palms facing out).

adult clothing. Children's dalmatics usually bear traces of having been taken up to allow a child to grow into them, and have been mended and patched as well (see figure 16).

The habits of Christian monks were plain and simple, often made by the monks themselves in monastic weaving establishments. A monk's clothing consisted of one tunic-like woolen garment tied with a belt of braided coir fibers. A monk's level in the hierarchy of the church was indicated by various types of stoles and how they were wrapped. Vestments for priests and deacons were modeled on earlier Greek and Roman garment types, but became more elaborate during the course of this period. The *colobium*, for example, was the first dress of Christian deacons, who later changed to the dalmatic as it became the common mode of male dress.

16. A child's dalmatic with two clavi *having leaf-shaped pendants and cuff-bands decorated with stylized vegetal motifs. It is tapestry-woven with wool threads dyed red, blue, yellow, and black, applied to plainwoven undyed linen in which thicker warp threads create white-on-white stripes.*

Size, 52 cm long (originally longer, but shortened at the waist by a tuck; also patched at the shoulders). Umayyad or later (?). Provenience unknown. CMNH *10309-92.*

At the close of Egypt's Byzantine period, there was a brief time when, for less than one generation, Egypt was under Persian rule. The Persian invasion of Egypt appears to have introduced new designs. This is particularly evident in one type of wall hanging wherein figures, usually in Persian costume, are arranged within columnar structures (see figure 17). Thus, the fashions of hostile lands bordering the Empire had

17. A wall hanging fragment with a portion of a male torso with upraised hand. Part of a ribbon appears below the figure. This piece is tapestry-woven with wool threads dyed tan, brown, black, and with red warp and background.

Size, 33.5 × 11.4 cm. Umayyad. Provenience unknown. CMNH 10061-157.

a great impact on Egyptian textiles, as did increased international commerce and trade. The internationalism of Egypt's textile industry continued after Egypt was no longer a part of the Byzantine Empire.

The Arab Dynasties

The Islamic calendar begins in A.D. 622 with the year A.H. 1 (*anno hegirae*, that is, the year after the migration of the prophet from Mecca to Medina).

The prophet's countrymen and followers from the nomadic tribes of Arabia soon began to build the new political and religious superpower of the Middle East, and much of the Byzantine Empire, including Egypt, became part of the Islamic world.

Islamic Influences.   At first, Byzantine textile-manufacturing techniques, designs, and garment types continued without radical change. During the first few centuries, figural representations adorned fabrics despite Koranic injunctions against such images (see figures 18 and 19). Over time, however, increasing international trade and the introduction of Islamic religion and customs profoundly influenced the preexisting Byzantine and Christian textile traditions which had, in turn, transformed their Pharaonic, Greek, and Roman antecedents. Garment types based on the tunic gradually died out as a growing urban middle class dressed in new fashions more in keeping with Islamic mores. Women, for example, began to cover their heads and bodies with many layers of clothing, but their fashions changed less than men's, probably reflecting women's relatively secluded and protected status. Trousseau lists describing the complete wardrobe of the later medieval Egyptian bride indicate that prosperous Jewish, Christian, and Moslem women all seem to have brought the same types of garments in their dowries. Measures were sporadically introduced, however, to regulate for Christians and Jews a dress distinctive from that of the Muslims.

Textile Manufacture.   As for the textile industry, the early Arab dynasties had inherited a profitable system of factories and trade in Egyptian textiles. Successive rulers in Egypt greatly strengthened controls on production and trade even as they enlarged the country's

18. *A well-preserved wall hanging fragment with a stylized version of the Pharaonic Egyptian sphinx below a pearl border. It is tapestry-woven with wool threads dyed brown, yellow,* *orange, red, dark blue, and blue-green (background).*

Size, 18 × 18.3 cm. Umayyad. Provenience unknown. CMNH 10061-151.

most important industry. During the early Arab dynasties, the preexisting Egyptian textile centers became more specialized (see figure 20). Alexandria continued to produce silk and linen, and continued to enjoy uninterrupted trade with North Africa (Ifrikiya) and the Maghreb, Spain, Byzantium, and Rome. (In a turnabout, India began to import cloth from Egypt: Alexandrian tiraz, a new type of garment decoration, described below, and linens were bestowed upon honored

19. A less well-preserved fragment with a stylized sphinx below a jewel and pearl border. It is tapestry-woven with wool threads dyed blue, yellow, red, and blue-green (background), and may be from the same wall hanging as shown in figure 18.

Size, 20 × 30 cm. Umayyad. Provenience unknown. CMNH 10061-292.

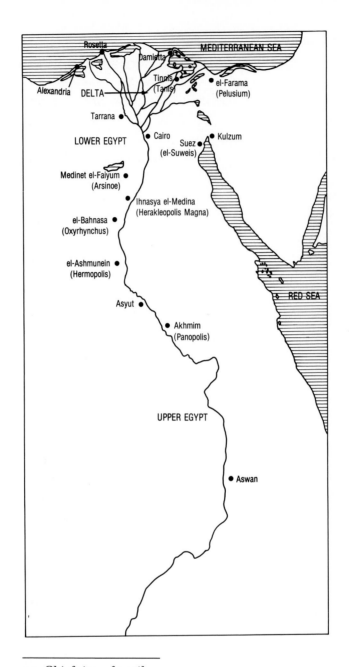

20. *Chief sites of textile*
manufacture and commerce
during the Arab dynasties.

individuals by the sultan of Delhi.) The centers in Lower Egypt were known primarily for linen, which was the most important branch of the textile industry. Damietta was known for its fine linens, or sharb, only in white and sometimes interwoven with gold threads, and its tiraz. Tinnis was known for dyed linens, furnishings of every kind, towels, Greek brocades, tiraz, and Kaaba coverings (also described below).

These famed textiles from Damietta and Tinnis were sent to the court at Baghdad and were also traded with the other territories of Byzantium. Westerners venerated silks that came from the Byzantine emperors, who had, in turn, acquired them from trade with Egypt under Arab Islamic rule. "The results were sometimes comical," wrote La Barre Starensier (1982: 450). "The textile venerated as the veil of St. Anne, the object of pilgrimages to Vaucluse, was a Fatimid cloth with profane images of sphinxes and a heathen [sic] Arabic inscription in silk identifying the object as the product of the Damietta tiraz."

South of the Delta and the Faiyum, the major centers were fewer and farther between but still they captured international reknown for their linens, cottons, and wools (used for veils, garments, and carpets). Cairo was known for its brocades, silks, and tiraz factories. Centers in Upper Egypt were known for their wools, and Aswan, in particular, was famous for its tents.

In taking over the preexisting industrial and commercial network, Arab private and state textile manufacturing enterprises continued to employ the same weavers: the local inhabitants called, by the Arabs, Qibt (from the Greek *Aigyptioi*, from which we derive the term "Copt" designating a Christian Egyptian). "Qibt" means "Egyptian" but implies no distinction as to race or religion other than not Arab or Islamic.

The weavers worked under grim conditions, earning extremely low wages and relegated to the lowest end of the social spectrum. In addition, the textile workers had to rent the rooms they worked in and were heavily taxed.

Government controls were also tightened on what could be produced when and where. The controls began the moment the weaver sat down to work at his loom and continued until the fabric was finally bought. An official stamp had to be incorporated into each piece of cloth. As a result, all material bore the name of its quality (e.g., sharb linen) so the purchaser knew exactly what he was buying. Moreover, textiles were sold only through brokers appointed by the state, and government officials kept records of all transactions. Brokers and managers were directly accountable to the caliphs in this empire-wide network. Taxes were collected in cash and in kind (i.e., textiles instead of money), and these revenues in kind were sold for money. Governments controlled the ports and had the choice, by purchase or confiscation, of whatever commodities might pass through them.

The Tiraz and the Kiswa. The strictest government controls concerned an extremely important new type of garment decoration, the tiraz. As we commonly use the term today, the tiraz was an inscribed arm band, a gift from the caliph worn as a badge of honor, favor, and distinction. The word "tiraz" originally meant embroidery, especially a robe with embroidered bands with writing on them. It came to mean an embroidered strip of writing, either woven or sewn, or any inscription on a band of any kind in any materials or technique (see figure 21). The inscriptions generally comprised Koranic verses or pious formulas and the names and

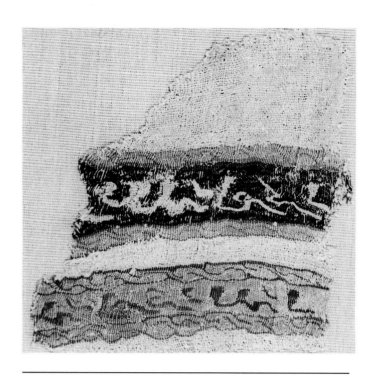

21. *A fragment of a tiraz with a repeated inscription in Arabic: "Victory comes from God." It is tapestry-woven with threads of undyed linen and perhaps* *silk dyed in red, yellow, and dark blue.*

Size, 9 × 8.5 cm. Fatimid. Provenience unknown. CMNH *10061-166.*

titles of the caliph. "Tiraz" was also used to designate the royal factories which manufactured such work and the operations of these factories. The word is of Persian origin, but the practice of bestowing special garments and cloths was an ancient one throughout the Middle East, mentioned in the Old Testament and Roman histories and, as we have seen, was an important Byzantine imperial practice. The most important precedent, however, seems to come from the beginning of Islamic history, when the Prophet gave his mantle to the poet Ka'b b. Zuhayr.

Twice each year the whole court in Egypt received new garments that were products of the state-owned tiraz factories in Alexandria, Tinnis, and Damietta. Tiraz were given to those in favor, that is, to those who had earned some kind of honor. (There were privately owned tiraz factories, too, but they were strictly controlled by the state, which dictated who could sell what to whom.) To medieval Middle Eastern bourgeoisie, royal tiraz garments were status symbols as well as valuable property, and clothing, in general, was still considered as an investment that was handed down from one generation to the next, and could be converted into cash if the need arose. Tiraz were also bestowed on a private level among Muslims, Christians, and Jews.

The earliest known tiraz were found in Egypt and the majority, by far, of all catalogued tiraz are also from Egypt. By the end of the Umayyad period, however, the tiraz system extended across the caliphate. There were tiraz factories in Palermo, Almeria, Seville, Granada, Malaga, Damascus, Antioch and, most important, Baghdad (see figure 2). Kazrun offers an example of Egypt's central place in tiraz production: It came to be called "the Damietta of Persia."

Another type of inscribed cloth has yielded valuable evidence for the historical importance of Egyptian textiles in Islam. All Muslim prayer is directed at the Kaaba, a small, square, stone building in the courtyard of the mosque in Mecca. Each mosque, wherever it is located, is designed to have a prayer niche (kibla) in a wall facing Mecca and the Kaaba. Covering the Kaaba—the focus of Islamic ritual—is the enormous kiswa cloth, traditionally of Egyptian manufac-

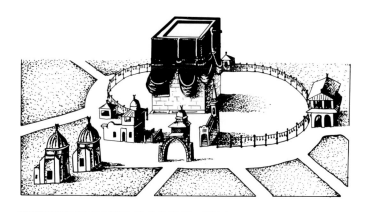

22. *An artist's copy of a Turkish lithograph showing the Kaaba (a small stone building in the mosque courtyard) at Istanbul in Ottoman times. The special fabric covering the Kaaba is the kiswa.*

ture (see figure 22). The right to cover the Kaaba originally belonged exclusively to the caliph who, each year since the Abbasid period, sent a kiswa of Egyptian manufacture. The Egyptian historian, Makrizi (A.D. 1364–1442/A.H. 766–845), described such cloths and their inscriptions in detail:

> I have seen on that part of the Kaaba which is next to the west corner, a cover which had inscribed on the upper part: "One of the things ordered by al-Sari ibn al-Hakim, and 'Abd al 'Aziz ibn Sahl Dhu'l-Riyasatain, and Tahir ibn al-Husain. Year 197 H. (812–13 A.D.)." I have also seen a piece of the Kubati [kiswa] of Egypt (Misr) in the midst of it (the covering?) except that they had written with a thin black line at the corners of the Temple: "One of the things which the Commander of the Faithful al-Ma'mun ordered. Year 206 H. (821–22 A.D.)." I have also seen one of Mahdi's coverings upon which was written: "In the name of God. Blessings

from God upon Abdallah al-Mahdi Muhammad, the Commander of the Faithful. May God prolong his existence. One of the things which Isma'il ibn Ibrahim ordered to be made in the tiraz factory of Tinnis, by the hand of al-Hakam ibn 'Ubaid, year 162 H. (778–79 A.D.)." (Serjeant, 1972: 146)

The tradition of covering the Kaaba is upheld to this day. Pieces of the used kiswa are regarded as holy and sold as relics to pilgrims.

In contrast to the rigidity of the tiraz system, the rulers of the Arab dynasties relaxed Byzantine restrictions on silk, and it became more commonly used for the clothing of private individuals and special furnishings. Linen and wool remained in widespread use for clothing and furnishings. It is important to note that the diffusion of techniques for cultivating silkworms, flax, and cotton spread at a rapid pace across the growing Islamic territories. Partly because of increased private trade with India, more cotton was in use (see figure 23). We know, again from literary sources, that a hugely expanded variety of materials were introduced into Egyptian textile manufacture and use. For example, mohair from the Levantine Angora goat entered the Egyptian repertory in the seventh century A.D. Serjeant (1972) mentions 166 names of textiles, usually known by their place of manufacture (not all of which were Egyptian). Sometimes these names are generic for a type of fabric originally produced elsewhere. Some have not yet been associated with actual remains. Others have found their way into contemporary Western usage: cotton, for example, derives from the Arabic *qutun*.

38 The thirteenth century marks the end of Egypt's central place in medieval textile manufacture and trade.

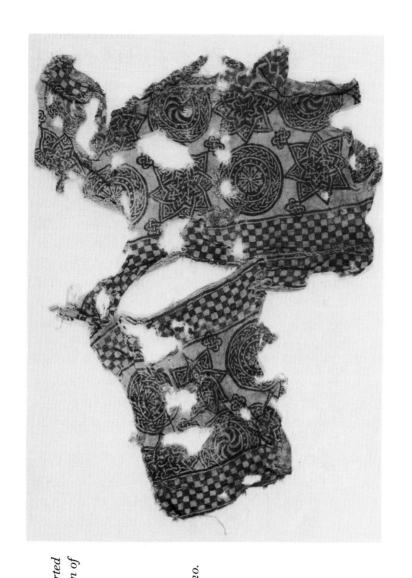

23. A wall hanging
fragment, probably imported
from India, with a pattern of
checks, stars, and circles
printed by the resist-dye*
method or stamped on
plainwoven cotton.

Size, 40 × 30 cm.
Mamluk (?). Provenience
unknown. CMNH 10061-220.

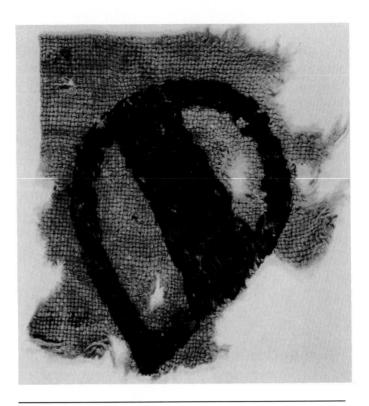

24. *A fragment with a*
shield-shaped heraldic
device (?) embroidered in*
silk—red with a blue
outline—on a plainwoven
background of undyed linen.

Size, 5.8 × 5 cm.
Mamluk (?). Provenience
unknown. CMNH *10061-211.*

Islamic lands came under attack by holy warriors from
western Europe, the crusaders. Sicilians burned Egyptian coastal towns in A.D. 1155/A.H. 533. Tinnis, which
at its height had had five thousand looms, was destroyed in A.D. 1227/A.H. 624 from fear that the Franks
might get possession of it. Damietta, which changed
hands several times between the Franks and the Muslims, was finally destroyed in the thirteenth century

A.D./seventh century A.H. by the Mamluks, again to eliminate its strategic importance (see figure 24). Textile production moved east, becoming a major industry in Turkey and Persia, from which areas rugs are still a valuable export commodity.

Appendix 1.
Chronology

Ancient Egypt
    Predynastic to Late period   ca. 4500–332 B.C.
    Ptolemaic period   ca. 332–30 B.C.
    Roman period   30 B.C.–A.D. 395

Byzantine period   A.D. 395–611
Persian period   A.D. 611–39
Byzantine reconquest   A.D. 639–41
Arab conquest   A.D. 641
    Caliphs of Medina   A.D. 632–61
    Umayyad caliphs of Damascus   A.D. 661–750
    Abbasid caliphs of Baghdad   A.D. 750–1258
    Tulunid governors of Egypt   A.D. 868–906
    Fatimid dynasty in Egypt   A.D. 969–1171
    Ayyubid dynasty in Egypt   A.D. 1171–1254
    Mamluk* dynasty in Egypt   A.D. 1254–1517
    Ottoman sultans of Turkey   A.D. 1560–1805

*Of Turkish origin.

Appendix 2.
Representative Textiles in the Carnegie Collection

This appendix contains additional examples from The Carnegie's collection of textiles from medieval Egypt. They were selected to illustrate further the range of styles and techniques used at that time. The sprang (diagonal intertwining, figure A-8) and tablet-woven band (figure A-9) are examples of comparatively rare pieces. A few items, such as the knitting (figures A-5 and A-6) and the tapestry cap (figure A-10), are not textiles in the strict sense of the word, because they were not woven on a loom. See the Glossary for explanations of techniques.

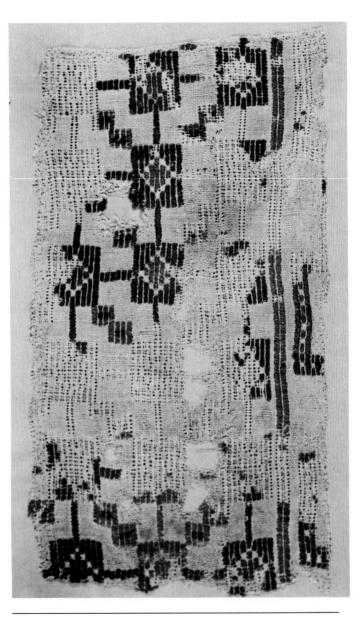

A-1. An unidentified fragment with a geometric brocade* ornamentation of lines linking diamonds in squares in looped wools dyed purple, red, and green on plainwoven undyed linen.

Size, 26 × 14.2 cm. Provenience unknown. CMNH 10061-159.

A-2. The main design on this unidentified fragment seems to represent the edge of a fringed, wind-blown sash decorated with variations on circular motifs. A small bird (?) is below. This cloth was doublewoven* (the same pattern appears in reverse on the back) on a drawloom* in wools dyed red, yellow, white, and green.

Size, 26 × 15 cm.
Provenience unknown.
CMNH *10061-233.*

*A-3. An unidentified
fragment with a repeating
pattern of geometric motifs
embroidered* in dark blue
wool on plainwoven undyed
linen, using the double
running stitch.*

*Size, 24 × 87 cm. (21.5 cm,
width of photographed
area). Provenience
unknown. CMNH 10309-87.*

A-4. An unidentified
fragment with palmettes on
either side of a vine
rinceau.* All motifs and
background are embroidered
in split and chain stitches in
red, white, brown, and
yellow dyed wools on a
background of plainwoven
undyed linen.

Size, 15 × 8 cm. Umayyad?
Provenience unknown.
CMNH 10061-213.

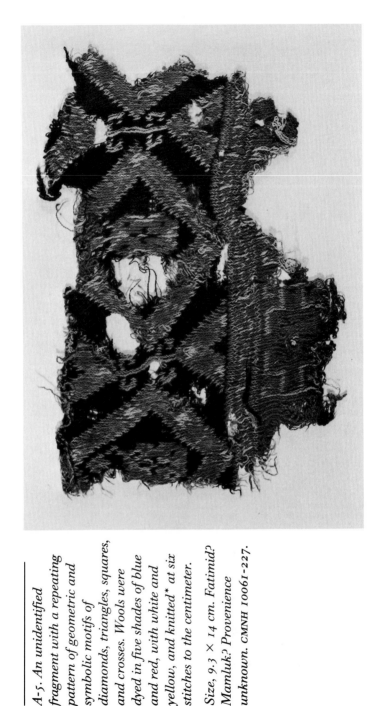

A-5. An unidentified
fragment with a repeating
pattern of geometric and
symbolic motifs of
diamonds, triangles, squares,
and crosses. Wools were
dyed in five shades of blue
and red, with white and
yellow, and knitted* at six
stitches to the centimeter.

Size, 9.3 × 14 cm. Fatimid?
Mamluk? Provenience
unknown. CMNH 10061-227.

A-6. A portion of a sock with a geometric pattern of stripes, zigzags, and diamonds knitted in undyed wools (background) and wools dyed light and dark blue. Note the jog in the pattern resulting from being knit as a tube.

Size, 9.5 × 18 cm. Mamluk (import from India). CMNH 10309-8.

A-7. An unidentified
fragment with repeating
design of rectangular panels
filled with geometric motifs.
Plainwoven in looped wools
dyed blue, red, yellow,
brown, and tan, cut to
form a pile.*

Size, 15 × 32 cm.
Provenience unknown.
CMNH 10061-244.

A-8. A portion of a band with geometric ornamentation of concentric diamonds diagonally intertwined in wools dyed red, green, yellow, and dark blue.

Size, 19 × 6 cm.
Provenience unknown.
CMNH 10061-221.

A-9. A portion of a
decorative band with a
tablet-woven* repeating
pattern of birds flanking a
tree, crosses in eight-pointed
stars flanking a column, and
unidentified motifs flanking

a palmette in red and yellow
wools, bordered by narrow
stripes in green wool.

Size, 25 × 4.8 cm.
Provenience unknown.
CMNH 10061-5.

A-10. A cap with concentric geometric designs around a central eight-pointed star, tapestry-woven* (on a form?) in undyed linen and wool dyed green, red, blue, and black. Currently split in numerous places, thus lying flat.

Size, 29 cm diameter. Mamluk? Provenience unknown. CMNH *10061-149.*

Glossary
by Deborah G. Harding

A textile is any woven fabric; that is, it is formed by interlacing one set of threads with another on a loom. (This is the strict, textbook definition. In common usage "textile" refers to any fabric.) This glossary presents some terms relating to textiles that may be helpful to the general reader. Words in capital letters are defined elsewhere in the Glossary.

Brocade. Brocade is made with an extra WEFT thread laid into the design area during the weaving process. It does not run all the way from SELVEDGE to selvedge, but turns back at the edge of its color area. It generally floats over the surface of the fabric, and is caught into it at intervals; hence, it is not part of the fabric structure, and if removed will leave a solid cloth with a pattern of holes. See appendix figure A-1.

Clavus. Clavus is a Latin word referring to the vertical stripes decorating Roman tunics. With or without additional attached medallions of various shapes, *clavi* extend over the shoulders of a tunic from front to back. Many were purple, but multicolored *clavi* were made as well. They could be woven in or sewn on after the garment was assembled. See figures 10 and 13 in the text.

Doubleweave. Two layers of WARPS or WEFTS (or both) are used; pattern sections are interchanged from one face of the fabric to the other, making a reversible fabric. Thus, where one side will show, for example, a red tree on a yellow ground, the other side will show a yellow tree on a red ground. Both TABBY and TWILL doubleweaves are found in the post-Pharaonic textiles in the Carnegie collection. The majority are weft-faced and may use three colors at a time. Because of their complexity, these fabrics were often woven on DRAWLOOMS. See appendix figure A-2.

Drawloom. See *Looms.*

Dyes. Deep and vibrant colors were obtained in medieval Egypt primarily from vegetable sources. Mordants, which are chemical agents added to fix the dye to the fiber, also affected the color, with different mordants producing different colors from the same dye bath. Alum was the most common mordant, although iron acetate (made from iron and vinegar) and iron sulphate (occurring as an impurity in alum) were also used.

Shades of red were obtained from alkanet root *(Alkanna tinctoria)* and madder root *(Rubia tinctorum)*. Madder can produce shades from pink to purplish-brown, depending on the mordant and the temperature of the dye bath. A nonvegetable source for red was the dried bodies of the female kermes *(Kermes vermilio)*, an insect living on certain evergreen oaks of northern Africa and southeastern Europe. Henna may also have been used.

A blue dye was derived from fermented leaves of the woad plant *(Isatis tinctoria)*. By dyeing fiber blue with woad, then top-dyeing red with madder or alkanet, purple was produced. Top-dyeing deeper blues and reds yielded dark brown or even black.

Yellow may have been derived from safflower *(Carthamus tinctorius)*, which would not, however, have been particularly desirable because it is water-soluble and can be washed away. Iron buff was also used for yellow. Green was produced by top-dyeing yellow over blue.

A method called "resist dyeing" prevents the cloth from accepting the dye. A material such as melted wax is painted onto the areas to remain undyed. The remainder is painted with a mordant to make the dyes fast, and the whole piece is dipped in the dye. When the wax is removed, a color scene or design appears on a natural, undyed ground. See figure 23 in the text.

Embroidery. Embroidery is a form of decorative sewing done with needle and thread after a fabric is woven. The Egyptian fabrics in The Carnegie collection have embroidery using the satin stitch, the double running stitch (also known as the "Holbein," "blackwork," or "double darning" stitch), and the split stitch.

The satin stitch (figure a) is a simple, straight, flat stitch in which the stitches are made parallel and touching each other to completely fill an area and create a smooth surface; the back is identical to the front. The double running stitch (figure b) is also a straight, flat stitch, made by running a line of stitches of equal length on both faces and then filling in the gaps by reversing the direction. It is used for outlines, and is

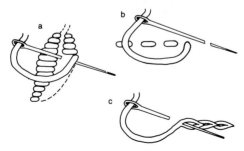

identical on both faces. In split stitch, as its name suggests, each new stitch is made through and splits the previous stitch. this creates more texture than the other two stitches; it is used for both outlines and filling (figure c). See figure 24 in the text and appendix figures A-3 and A-4.

Flying shuttle. This is a second shuttle, carrying an extra WEFT thread, usually used with TAPESTRY weave. It is free from the normal constraints of the horizontal passage of the main shuttle. In interlaced medallions, the flying shuttle weft forms the whole design on a solid background. The extra weft, usually in a contrasting color, may be used to soften a stepped outline into a curve (figure a), and often has the effect of making the figure stand out from the background. Flying shuttle is also used in shading and highlights, as well as minute details. It follows the same TABBY over-and-under path as the main shuttle.

Another stitch, the soumak stitch, may also be done with the flying shuttle. The weft thread encircles each WARP or group of warp threads and then floats over the surface before wrapping another warp (figure b). It may proceed horizontally, vertically, or diagonally as the design requires. See figures 4, 7, and 13 in the text.

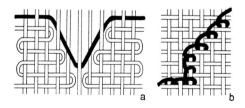

a   b

Knitting. Knitting is formed by a single thread in a series of loops held on a needle with a blunt point on one or both ends. A second needle pulls a new loop through each old loop in succession as it removes them from the first needle. The work can be done back and forth in flat rows or around in a closed circle. See appendix figures A-5 and A-6.

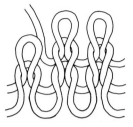

Looms. Egyptian looms, as depicted in tomb paintings and models, were of two types: an upright loom (figure a), similar to modern tapestry looms, and a horizontal ground loom (figure b), whose modern descendant was used, with little change, well into the twentieth century for rug weaving. Very sophisticated techniques could be performed on this simple equipment.

The drawloom, introduced from the East in post-Pharaonic times, made the weaving of intricate patterns quick and mechanical, by allowing control over individual threads. A loop with a long tail was tied around each WARP thread; the tails were joined in groups to leashes according to the pattern to be woven. By pulling the leashes in order, the pattern was formed with no more effort on the weaver's part than was necessary to weave a plain cloth (figure c). See appendix figure A-2.

Pile. Pile is formed by loops of a supplemental WARP or WEFT drawn up during the weaving process, usually on thin rods which are later withdrawn. The resulting pile may be cut or left uncut. The fragment in appendix figure A-7 has uncut pile. Velvet, velveteen, terry cloth, and most "Oriental" rugs are examples of pile weaving. Hooked rugs are a form of pile that is added to a foundation cloth after weaving.

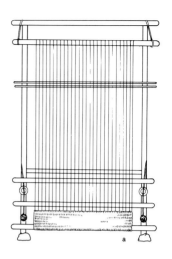

a

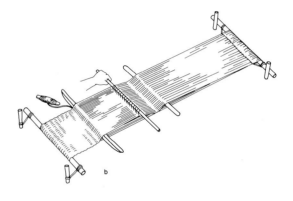

b

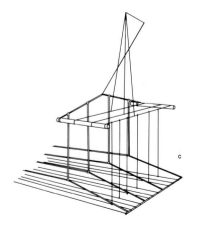

c

Rinceau. Rinceau is a French word meaning foliage and is used to describe a decorative motif of scrolls made with vines and leaves.

Selvedge ("self-edge"). The smooth, uncut edge of a fabric where the WEFT threads have been turned back into the weave is called a selvedge. A selvedge may be reinforced with extra or thicker threads for strength. Vertical LOOMS can create fabrics with four selvedges, weaving right to the ends of the WARP threads.

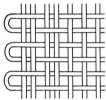

Sprang. Sprang includes several techniques in which the parallel WARP threads are manipulated to form a fabric without the addition of WEFT threads. Since the warp is fastened at both ends, mirror-image structures appear at the ends, and the work is finished in the middle. The types of sprang appearing in the Carnegie collection are interlinking (interlacing) and intertwining.

Both forms involve twisting the threads around their neighbors, with subsequent rows locking in the twists of the previous row. In interlinking (figure a), adjacent threads are twisted around each other to form an elastic mesh. In intertwining (figure b), pairs of threads are twisted around and enclose neighboring threads

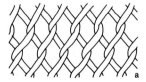

or groups of threads to form a more solid and less-elastic fabric. See figure 8 in the text and appendix figure A-8.

Tabby weave (plainweave, checkweave). Tabby weave is simple over-one-thread, under-one-thread interlacement. Most modern factory-made fabrics, especially prints, are tabby-woven. All of the ancient Egyptian weaves were variations of tabby weave. See appendix figure A-4.

Tablet weaving (card weaving). Tablet weaving uses small flat tablets or cards, usually square with a hole in each corner, through which the WARP ends are threaded. The cards are turned, in groups or individually, to raise and lower the threads during the weaving process. A great amount of control over the pattern is achieved in this way, similar to that of the DRAWLOOM. See appendix figure A-9. However, since the cards are turned by hand, the fabric is restricted to a relatively narrow width by the size of the weaver's hands.

The finished fabric structure is different from that produced on an ordinary LOOM. As the tablets are turned, the warp ends threaded through each card twist around each other into cords and untwist again if the pattern is reversed. This process forms a denser, firmer fabric than a similar pattern woven on a drawloom, making tablet weaving especially suitable for decorative trim, horse and camel gear, and belts—wherever a firm, narrow band is needed.

Tapestry. Tapestry is a WEFT-faced TABBY WEAVE in which the weft threads are confined to their particular color area, and do not necessarily travel from edge to edge of the cloth. Unlike BROCADE, the pattern thread is also a structural thread, so changes in color can result in gaps and slits in the fabric. Various types of joins are used to prevent weakening of the fabric with long slits at color changes.

The toothed join (figure a) is made by turning weft threads alternately around a common WARP thread. A variant, the dovetail join (figure b), turns the threads around a common warp end in groups of two or more. Interlocked joins (figure c) are made by linking together each thread with its neighbor of the adjacent color between the warp threads. This join is less efficient to make than the dovetail, but is less obtrusive in the design. See appendix figure A-10.

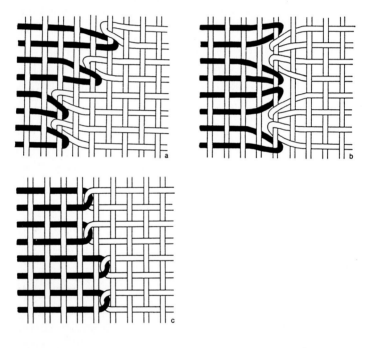

Twill. Twill is an interlacing in which a thread passes over and under more than one thread at a time, for example, over two and under two, or over three and under one. The starting point of the interlacement is offset by at least one thread in each new row; this forms a characteristic diagonal line in the fabric. Denim is an example of a modern twill fabric.

Warp. The warp consists of the lengthwise threads stretched ("warped") on the loom and manipulated to permit the passage of the WEFT. The textile is *warp-faced* when warp threads are so closely set as to totally cover the weft threads.

Weft (woof, filling). The weft consists of the crosswise threads inserted in the WARP during weaving. A textile is *weft-faced* when weft threads are so closely set as to totally cover the warp threads. TAPESTRY is a weft-faced weave.

Suggested Reading

Bowman, A. *Egypt After the Pharaohs: 332 BC–AD 642 from Alexander to the Arab Conquest.* Berkeley: The University of California Press, 1986.

Ettinghausen, R. and O. Grabar. *The Art and Architecture of Islam.* Baltimore and Middlesex: Penguin Books Ltd., 1987.

Hall, R. *Egyptian Textiles.* Aylesbury: Shire Publications Ltd., 1986.

Houston, M. G. *Ancient Greek, Roman, and Byzantine Costume and Decoration.* London: Adams and Charles Black, 1947.

Mango, C. *The Art of the Byzantine Empire: 312–1453.* Sources and Documents in the History of Art, edited by H.W. Janson. Englewood Cliffs, N.J.: Prentice-Hall, Inc., 1972.

Riefstahl, E. *Patterned Textiles in Pharaonic Egypt.* Brooklyn: The Brooklyn Museum and The Brooklyn Institute of Arts and Sciences, 1945.

Roth, H.L. *Ancient Egyptian and Greek Looms.* 2nd ed. Halifax: F. King and Sons, 1951.

Trilling, J. *The Roman Heritage: Textiles from Egypt and the Eastern Mediterranean, 300–600 A.D.* The Textile Journal, vol. 21. Washington D.C.: The Textile Museum, 1982.

Weibel, A.C. *Two Thousand Years of Textiles.* New York: Pantheon Books on behalf of the Detroit Institute of Arts, 1952.

Bibliography

The Antinoopolis Papyri. Part II. London: Egypt Exploration Society, 1950.

Esin, Emel (Tek). *Mecca the Blessed, Madinah the Radiant.* New York: Crown Publisher, Inc. 1963.

Gayet, A. *Antinoë et les sépultures de Thaïs et Sérapion.* Paris: Société Française d'Éditions d'Art, 1902.

Hunt, A.S., and C.C. Edgar. *Select Papyri. Volume I, Private Affairs.* Loeb Classical Library. London and New York: G.P. Putnam's Sons, 1932.

La Barre Starensier, A. *An Art Historical Study of the Byzantine Silk Industry.* Ann Arbor: University Microfilms, 1982 (Columbia Dissertation, 1982).

Mango, C. *The Art of the Byzantine Empire: 312–1453.* Sources and Documents in the History of Art, edited by H.W. Janson. Englewood Cliffs, N.J.: Prentice-Hall, Inc., 1972.

Pharr, C. *The Theodosian Code and Novels and the Sirmondian Constitutions: A Translation with Commentary, Glossary and Bibliography.* Princeton: Princeton University Press, 1952.

Serjeant, R.B. *Islamic Textiles: Material for a History of Islamic Textiles up to the Mongol Conquest.* Beirut: Librairie du Liban, 1972.

Stillman, Y.K. *Female Attire of Medieval Egypt According to the Trousseau Lists and Cognate Material from Cairo Geniza.* Ann Arbor: University Microfilms, 1973 (University of Pennsylvania Dissertation, 1972).

Acknowledgments

Front cover. Photo by Stanley W. Lantz.

Fig. 1. From Gayet, A. *Antinoë et les sépultures de Thaïs et Sérapion.* Paris: Société Française d'Éditions d'Art, 1902.

Figs. 2, 5, and 20. Maps drawn by Linda A. Witt.

Figs. 3, 14, and 15. From Houston, Mary G. *Ancient Greek, Roman, and Byzantine Costume and Decoration.* London: A&C Black, 1947.

Figs. 4, 6–10, 12, 13, 16–19, 21, 23, 24, and all Appendix photos. Carnegie Museum of Natural History photos by Stanley W. Lantz.

Fig. 11. Drawing by Linda A. Witt. Adapted from Wessel, K. *Coptic Art.* New York: McGraw-Hill Publishing Co., 1965; used by permission.

Fig. 22. Drawing by Linda A. Witt. Adapted from a Turkish lithograph after E. Sabri, *Mir'at i-Mekke.*

Glossary drawings by Linda A. Witt. The drawloom was adapted from a drawing by A.A.M. Chowanetz in Broudy, E. *The Book of Looms.* New York: Van Nostrand Reinhold Co., 1979.